# The first Christmas

Story by Penny Frank
Illustrated by John Haysom

THE LION
STORY BIBLE
32

TRING · BATAVIA · SYDNEY

The Bible tells us
how God sent his Son Jesus to show
us what God is like and how we can
belong to God's kingdom.
This is the story of when God's
Son was born.
You can find the story in your own
Bible, in the first chapters of the
Gospels of Matthew and Luke.

Copyright © 1986 Lion Publishing

Published by
**Lion Publishing plc**
Icknield Way, Tring, Herts, England
ISBN 0 85648 757 0
**Lion Publishing Corporation**
1705 Hubbard Avenue, Batavia,
Illinois 60510, USA
ISBN 0 85648 757 0
**Albatross Books Pty Ltd**
PO Box 320, Sutherland, NSW 2232, Australia
ISBN 0 86760 541 3

First edition 1986
Reprinted 1987

Printed and bound in Hong Kong

**British Library Cataloguing in
Publication Data**

Frank, Penny
  The first Christmas. – (The Lion
Story Bible; v.32)
  1. Jesus Christ – Nativity – Juvenile
literature 2. Bible stories, English –
N.T.
  I. Title    II. Haysom, John
232.9'21    BT315.2

ISBN 0-85648-757-0

**Library of Congress
Cataloging-in-Publication Data**

Frank, Penny.
The first Christmas.
(The Lion Story Bible; 32)
1. Jesus Christ—Nativity—Juvenile
literature. [1. Jesus Christ—
Nativity. 2. Bible stories—N.T.]
I. Haysom, John, ill. II. Title.
III. Series: Frank, Penny. Lion Story
Bible; 32.
BT315.2.F72 1986    226'.09505
85-24089
ISBN 0-85648-757-0

Long ago, before the first Christmas, there was a beautiful young woman called Mary.

She lived in the little town of Nazareth.

4

One day, when Mary was busy in her home, the room was suddenly full of bright light.

There, in the light, stood an angel of God. Mary was really frightened.

'Don't be afraid, Mary,' said the angel. 'The message I have for you is a message of joy. You are going to have a baby son.'

'But I have no husband,' said Mary.

'He will be the Son of God himself,' said the angel. 'You must call him Jesus.'

'I will do whatever God wants,' said Mary, and the angel went away.

There was a young man in Nazareth, called Joseph. He loved Mary. He wanted Mary to marry him.

The angel visited Joseph, in a dream.

'I have come to tell you that Mary is going to have a baby. He is the Son of God,' said the angel.

'You must call the baby, Jesus. He has come to save the whole world.'
Then the angel went away.

Mary and Joseph made their plans to get married. They loved each other very much. They often talked about the angel's message and about the special baby.

'Will people believe that Jesus is the Son of God?' said Mary.

'Don't worry,' Joseph said. 'Some people will understand. God promised he would send a special person to rescue the world. Now we can be glad that he has kept his promise.'

So Joseph and Mary waited for Jesus
to be born. There were a lot of things
to get ready for the baby. It seemed
a long time to have to wait.

One day they heard that the Emperor
who ruled their country had made
a new law.

'Everyone must travel back to his
home town to have his name written on
a register,' Joseph told Mary. 'We will
have to go all the way to Bethlehem.'

'I would have liked to stay at home
to have my baby, but the prophets did
say that God's Son would be born in
Bethlehem,' said Mary, as the donkeys
carried them on their journey.

'I am so tired,' she said. 'And it
is such a long way.'

When they came to the town, it was very busy. So many people had come to register in Bethlehem that there was no room left in the inn.

But the innkeeper said they could use the stable where he kept his animals.

Joseph helped Mary down from the donkey and took her into the stable. Mary made a bed for them on the straw with her warm cloak. She knew her baby would soon be born.

When the baby was born, they wrapped him up warmly and made a place for him to sleep in the manger, where the animals' hay was kept.

'His name is Jesus,' they said. 'He is God's own Son.'

The animals stood watching them. Their warm breath filled the tiny stable.

It was not quiet for very long.
The stable door creaked open and some shepherds came in.

'Where is the baby?' they asked Joseph gently. 'Can we see him?'

'Of course,' said Joseph. 'But how did you know a baby had been born?'

'We were out on the hills with our sheep,' said the shepherds. 'Suddenly there was a bright light and God's angels came to us. They told us there was a baby here who would grow up to save us all. And we came at once to find him.'

The shepherds went back to their sheep. They told their story to everyone they met.

Mary and Joseph stayed in Bethlehem for a while.

One day there was a knock on the door. Some important visitors stood outside.

'We have come a long way to see the baby king,' the wise men said. 'Is he really in here?'

'Yes,' said Joseph. 'But how did you know a baby had been born?'

'We saw a bright star in the sky,' they
said. 'Our books showed us it would lead
us to the baby born to be a king
in Israel. So we followed it.'

The visitors knelt down by the baby
and presented their gifts of gold,
frankincense and myrrh.

When the visitors had gone, Joseph and Mary looked at their baby. They had so much to think about.

They remembered the angels who had come to the shepherds, and the bright star which had led the wise men.

They looked again at the beautiful presents.

'At last God has sent his Son to Israel,' said Joseph.

'Yes,' said Mary, 'to Israel and to the whole world. Those wise men came from far away. Maybe they need him there too.'

Joseph and Mary thanked God for the baby Jesus. They knew that God had kept his promise to send his Son to save the whole world.

They did not understand yet what work God had for Jesus to do. But they knew that he would show the world what God is like.

**The Lion Story Bible** is made up of 52 individual stories for young readers, building up an understanding of the Bible as one story — God's story — a story for all time and all people.

The New Testament section (numbers 31–52) covers the life and teaching of God's Son, Jesus. The stories are about the people he met, what he did and what he said. Almost all we know about the life of Jesus is recorded in the four Gospels — Matthew, Mark, Luke and John. The word gospel means 'good news'.
    The last four stories in this section are about the first Christians, who started to tell others the 'good news', as Jesus had commanded them — a story which continues today all over the world.

The story of *The First Christmas* comes from the New Testament, Matthew's Gospel chapter 1, and Luke's Gospel chapters 1 and 2. God's special spokesmen, the Old Testament Prophets, looked forward to the time when God would send the Messiah, a king of peace, to rescue his people. Through the long centuries God's people clung to this promise, while their land was conquered first by the Greeks, then by the Romans. It became the province of Judea, with a puppet king (Herod) under the rule of the Roman Emperor Augustus. Then, at last, God stepped in to fulfil his promise. Without pomp or fuss God's Son was born, in a stable in Bethlehem.
    The next book in the series, number 33: *When Jesus was young*, tells the story of Jesus' boyhood.